SMALL
NUCLEAR
FAMILY

SMALL NUCLEAR FAMILY

👓 EYEWEAR PUBLISHING

MEL
PRYOR

First published in 2015
by Eyewear Publishing Ltd
74 Leith Mansions, Grantully Road
London W9 1LJ
United Kingdom

Cover design and typeset by Edwin Smet
Author photograph by portraits by Sarah
Printed in England by TJ International Ltd, Padstow, Cornwall

The right of Mel Pryor to be identified as author of
this work has been asserted in accordance with section 77
of the Copyright, Designs and Patents Act 1988

ISBN 978-1-908998-82-8

*Eyewear wishes to thank Jonathan Wonham for his very generous patronage of our press;
as well as our other patrons and investors who wish to remain anonymous.*

WWW.EYEWEARPUBLISHING.COM

for Peter, Rose and Ed

Mel Pryor grew up in England and Hong Kong.
She studied history at Durham University and
trained as a solicitor. Her poetry has been widely
published and her pamphlet *Drawn on Water*
was published by Eyewear in 2014. She lives in
Hertfordshire with her husband and two children.

Table of Contents

Part I

Gorilla — 10

Via del Corso — 11

Because I will be more American — 12

Hokusai — 14

Overseas — 15

The Cam — 17

Walking the River Tay — 19

Rattus Rattus — 20

Fight and flight — 21

Mosquito — 22

Spring Birth — 26

Orthopaedic Surgeon — 28

Three train stops from St. Francis Comprehensive — 29

My Ex-boyfriend — 30

Sciophobia — 31

Eating ciabatta in a North London café six days after the bombs — 32

Missing — 35

Search — 36

Maurice, Gone — 37

Imposter — 39

Poet-cat — 40

Naming the cat — 41

Part II

After the business of oversleeping, I apologise — 44
Your girlfriend's red leather jacket — 45
Hanbury Street — 46
St Bride's — 47
Song — 49
Wedding Gift — 50
Rose — 51
The Eurythmics play 'Thorn in My Side' — 52
The Waterboys play 'The Whole of the Moon' — 53
Emergency Birth — 54
Heritage Dive — 55
Back — 56
Mr Rice — 57
Space — 58
Family Man — 59
Loft — 60
Star Watch — 61
Housework — 62
Alder — 64
Sighting seals on a beach in the Farne Islands — 65
The Swan Hellenic Cruise — 66
October — 67

Notes — 69
Acknowledgements — 71

the houses are murmuring with many small
pockets of emotion

— Denise Riley, 'Affections must not'

Part I

Gorilla

You could sense expectation, the kids at the cage
after the whole King Kong experience,
a pecs-bashing, jungle titan performance
from the attraction, sprawled across the floor
like a discarded coat. A crowd of boys
plopped mints like mothballs through the bars, to lure
a look, a rise; the body lumbering,
on hands and knees it seemed, to centre stage,
the beaten stance and cowed, obedient eyes
still holding their magnificence. I thought
I'd found a new dawn of Darwin, I thought
I'd found the origin of suffering,
would've put my cheek against his long malaise,
said brother, forefather, I *know* what this is.

Via del Corso

Rather than go over all that again,
let's go back to Rome, tenacious,
optimistic Rome, where twelve years married
we roomed opposite a florist's shop
in the Albergo Santa Chiara,
woke for four short dawns only
in April's slatted light. Mostly we were happy
in Rome. I was animated,
you wore your honeymoon shoes,
and the day it rained, it didn't rain for long.

Throw the window open
and there again's the distant scent
of *rosa, pisello odoroso, caprifoglio,*
bouquets in buckets down the street.
Let's revisit the scene in Piazza Navona
where over scoops of *gelato sette veli*
you leaned in close, asked, chivalrous
and serious, for 'Just one more child.'
Let's take the bitten light of a nectarine,
the last bus to Trastevere, alight

lightheaded into buskers' song
and trudge the uphill path to Tasso's tree.
We'll leave the baroque part where we argued,
wilding cats, mosquito bites, and take
only the general gist of it – easier for you,
I know, who lean Nero's tower-like
towards the positive. Today with you
I vow to remember most of Rome –
the Angelus, the softer bits of alabaster,
the Tiber running always through its centre.

Because I will be more American

we are driving across that great ocean
in a boat called Sea of Atlas, trying out
our new American voices.
I say downtown Minnesota, and aluminum,
you say freeway. I like the shape of freeway's vowels,
monophthong and diphthong juxtaposed.
I kiss you so you can taste the word again.
When I was eight, each week on TV Big Bird said
America, America, finite continent of the free.
Big Bird was strong and visual; he sang
and was never caged.
On his street I heard jacamars and grackles flap
their wings, pismires hymn a gubbinal.
When I was fifteen, Springsteen was on my wall,
his *brother in Khe Sahn, a woman in Saigon.*
America, I have my great grandfather's
San Franciscan dust in my cell structure,
I have his hair, I have his eyes, his sweet tooth,
I have his astigmatic vision of a bright
savannahed various place. Welcome me
into the state where he mapped routes
through elk tracks, earthquakes, tectonic bog.
America, I am journeying towards you;
soon I will unspool my new drawl
down the loops and splashes of the Sacramento River,
lay it in loping lines on the gold roads of Rodeo Drive,
the blush Californian boulevards
beside scrawled cement signatures.
America, I reject your Hollywood gods
but I'll take wilderness, canyons,
tallgrass prairies, the Mississippi's low refrain.

You ask me, my English love, to be more American
and I hold your pen in my small right
writing hand. See, on our map of this western
hemisphere's 16 trillion dollar corner
my pen can swirl from Eureka,
around the coast, the shorn
armpit of Apalachee Bay,
the Crater Lake of Oregon,
jink towards America's heart,
which is Manhattan's green statue,
or maybe Yale, or Harvard with its docents,
its napalm and its elevators.

Hokusai

Since he upped and left her and their son
for the printmaker in Tokyo,

I've noticed she curves forward slightly
like a tall Japanese wave breaching

the moment between rise and fall.
Her hands clasp and unclasp,

tremble a little like pink peonies
when the wind gets up over the valley.

Overseas

After the long birth like an opera
the baby, neckless, silent,
lifted from blood-arced sheets
and pumped into song by a sudden
audience of six and a breathing machine,
we took off to a foreign country
to catch our own breath, carrying
the languid bundle between us
and a shoulder of solid rucksack
packed with new clothes, toys, hope.

We arrived in the dry season, clocks
offbeat, day night and night day,
drove a hired Toyota to the ocean
where waves licked slow over plastic shoes
and up the hot pitted sand, so hot
the baby had to lie on cloth
until night's cool tread made blood
flow faster through its shallows. Her suck
weakened and we fed her milk,
drop on drop from our fingers.

All I wanted was a smile, for her to turn
when she heard my voice,
but even the girls carrying huge fruit
in baskets, their beaded hair sculpted
into plaits of black elaborate wheat,
couldn't coax a look or shift of eye,
bright as the sun behind its glaze.
They shook elephant earlobes, kissed
the fontanelle and threaded

leather bracelets round her wrists.
Months on I did her hair like a native,
never set her down because her spine
seemed cotton-stitched, because she cried,
cried all night with mosquito insistence
as if noise was the imperfect's weapon
against the strong, though once she made a fist
with one hand. I asked if we could go home,
but you said, no, no we couldn't return,
there was still so much for us to see,
so many beautiful palaces for us to visit.

The Cam

But then I knew nothing of these waters,
or how to manoeuvre through heavy
summer river traffic, where a hand
might take my hand to help me on board,
and then let go, leave only a spruce pole,
a stomach-pivot, my flawed sense of balance
to propel the flat-nosed boat: so Nicky and I,
three children between us, hired a puntsman
and punt, a guided tour of the Cam
for one hot afternoon's hour. The children
sprawled in the bottom of the punt; I sat
semi-upright beside Nicky, upper back
supported by scrubs-green cushions,
Keds kicked off, toes stretched out before me,
as sockless as Dad on his deathbed.
Ahead – the boltless Mathematical bridge,
to our right, Queen's, King's College,
to our left, St John's clockless clock tower;
or so our chauffeur told us, beautiful
student of history from Sheffield
working the river for one summer only.
For me he punted us fifty three years
downstream, to find my father here again
over on the tilting bank's ochre grass –
eighteen years old, dressed as in his photograph
in corduroy trousers and woollen tie,
grey eyes curious for love and the root
of all things, arms, stance, perhaps
a little awkward. The punt turned
180 degrees. There was barely a breath
on the water. He was seven days dead,

Dad, who'd believed in the true laws of evolution,
the persistence of genes, forgiveness of sins,
the first raw assault of a division of cells.
The bruise brown water was cold
under my fingers. To our right,
St John's clockless clock tower,
to our left, King's, Queen's College, ahead –
the Mathematical bridge. Nicky and I
spoke only of architecture. The children
sprawled in the bottom of the punt,
too full of light and afternoon to notice
each blithe inhalation and exhalation.

Walking the River Tay

What were you thinking of? – living on alcohol
and the ebullition of soluble paracetamol
for so long – years! – years trailing cirrhotic fuel
pumped through the Co-op's strongest 8 for 6 brown ale
or something cruel like the blackcurrant diesel
that had you manhandled from the Glover's Needle,
mouth still puckered round a bottle's dilated pupil.
Me, I'd sooner have a coke can's just-pulled pluming nostril,
or something watered down, something sensible
knowing that, unlike you, I was no immortal,

which brings me to the night I watched you vomit, shamble
onto the parapet sixty metres above river level
and breast its skinny metal girth at a casual amble.
You stopped, peered up the eye of your empty bottle
like a telescope, then kept on going, only a light drizzle
and the constellations as your night-air handrail,
only my mindless panicked chat to keep your hot head cool
the whole damn distance to the water's cut-off wall.
What would it have taken – a dropped star? – for you to fall?
You held glass like faith and lived to hear the tale.

Rattus Rattus

A rat, dead in a pool of grime by the bin,
had me in tears and screaming. I was eight
and this my initiation into death.
'Too much noise,' my amah said. 'Go out,
go out, *sau seng, sau seng.*' The toothpick teeth,
eye blobs creaming in the Hong Kong heat,
and fly-swarm skimming the surface of a coat
as grubby as the gunk it mouldered in
haunted me for weeks. How brave the cat,
I thought, that conquered, put a stop to that.

Decades on I found its smaller twin
across the equator in a pool of shade,
looted of life and left at the boot room door.
The ormer ears were brushed with a pearl veneer
so clean you'd think the sea just washed them up.
It was the hand I touched — immaculate scrap
eight millimetres long, its fingers splayed
like the baby's in the five month scan,
the blurry photograph. How cruel the cat,
I thought, prinking beside the water butt.

Fight and flight

These endless days in bed have become absurd:
lining the mattress, sleepless, fractious... and now
my airless square has spawned a sudden fly
with warrior lungs and too much fighting instinct.
Fat as a truffle, he caulks the window's crack
with fly saliva, does a ping pong dance
so hard his fondant centre nearly pops.
Bang. Thwack. Farcical fool, the shame of you –
you think like sunlight you can pass through glass!
Dope-fly, don't worry, I won't flatten you.
Why would I when you have me out of bed
(at last, at last) ramming the window wide
to let the world, the sun, the wind come in
and you (goodbye, small fly, goodbye) fly out?

Mosquito

If you would see all of Nature gathered up at one point, in all her loveliness, and her skill, and her deadliness, and her sex, where would you find a more exquisite symbol than the Mosquito?
    – Havelock Ellis, 1920

A nip, unnoticed,
             becomes a hill, and the hill
(are there moles under my skin?)
          becomes…
               many hills!

I'm at one with the scenery, blending in well
with the region: the northern tip of my ear
supports a pike,
         the lobe two knolls,

and as for my hummocky ankle, my visible arm,
the back of my…

       Listen! Listen! Where's it from,

this soprano aria
     appassionato at moonfall
for my ear only?

  – A dust mote that's grown a woman's soul,
      an angel's pair of wings!

How seductively, enticingly
         she flips
(forwards, forwards) then

(vanished!)
                opens her mouth and sings.

Tiny Siren,
      Salome,
           now I see you
                      veil down and dancing

all floaty robes and incredible pins,
        tongue dripping with pathogens.

You look so frail,
        surely you come in peace.
Are you saying grace…
or some prayer
before Communion?

Here comes some mumble in my ear's confessional!
Am I to be your priest: should I grant absolution?

      No, you don't fool me,
you and your sisterhood,
                your heritage,
                        ma Cherie.

Don't for one moment think
I wouldn't put you to burn on a splinter,

hear you fizz
        like hair on coal
to erase
the last of your jazz,
the me-me-I whine of the entirely neurotic.

Everything you do is all about you.

How many lovers have you slurped, grown drunk on?
      How many turned sweaty, yellow, blue?

(Such injustice, how ironic, you alcoholic –
      that *their* mouths puked in a bucket,
their innocent livers were ruined.)

I hate your skinny beauty,
I hate your thighs,
your unambiguous sighs,
I hate your midnight binge.

      How many husbands, you smear,
you nymphomaniac spot
have you stolen?

Isn't every man a sucker for a filthy whisper in his ear?

And did you alight on *my* husband's skin,
was it *my* husband you sucked?

Such obscenity of trespass.
Such brawn,
such design.

Isn't he delicious? Isn't he sweet?
How many times did you savour the sticky texture
of his blood?

All I want to do is do you in.

I swat, I slap. I slap, I slap, I slap.

But it's my skin that's bruised,

and you glide off on the breeze I make for you
as if you own each updraft and no hand is a match
for your fragile agility.

My itching increases;
        my flailing fails.
You're the magician's assistant
who keeps coming back.

I wish you'd vanish.
        I wish I could saw you in half,
but you're too damn smart,
                you always win.

Spring Birth

Midnight, April, the Royal Infirmary.
Along the corridor someone is lulling
a baby to sleep,
someone is screaming.
I enter the damp meat smell
of the operating theatre
where the surgeon, stooped
over my wife's stripped lower body,
has made an incision
through her abdomen in the place
where I like to rest my ear
to hear the baby flutter
deep inside her, small
solitary seedling, hidden
from harm,
my wife's warmth worn on its skin.
Matcham said that fatherhood
must be at the core of the universe
and if I've been waiting for a day
all my life, this is it, my wife asleep,
about to give her greatest gift.
For years I've gathered up her life's anxieties,
dusted out her darkest rooms
and when she wept
I rocked her in my arms the way soon
I'll rock the small doll version of her
dressed in the little babygrow and shoes
I've left at home beside the cot.
Through the window owls like ghouls
circle the infirmary garden.
The surgeon lifts from my wife

a soggy soft lump.
But where the baby's mouth should be
is a beak.
Instead of feet – claws!
There are no ears, no hands,
no fingers, no arms;
and what is that mess of feathers
over the shoulders?
Bleak-faced, offensive,
it shakes out the moon in its bones,
half-lifts two wings behind it
as if straining for flight.
The beak opens to a glint of spit.
Cuck-oo, cuck-oo, cuck-oo,
its fledgling song, its birth cry.

Orthopaedic Surgeon

It was the way he strolled into that dun, welcome lounge
in a moss jumper like a liberal in combat trousers
with *the one* written all over his high, Renaissance face,
the way he took her eye with a medic's level appraisal
that stripped her zippered dress, her tights, her flesh,
the way he signed himself in with a biro flourish
as if writing his name on the rest of her night.
She was sure the crack in the paintwork mouth-height
behind him opened its lips a bit more, then more
when he smiled, extended his hand. Her heart's aorta
splintered. She thought she was an amputee.
She thought she was on amphetamines,
wanted to put her hooped ear like a stethoscope
to the left camber of his chest and the pulse below
while she stroked her flux and grip
into the arms, the legs, the impeccable fingers
she'd have squeezing the love out of her like bandages.

Three train stops from St. Francis Comprehensive

Fuckyou says he was eight when he got his first pube
twelve when he touched a girl's breast and with so much
success so young how come he can't now get laid
not even by minger Nadine from swimming club
whose pubes are more square than triangle down there and
I say lower the tone won't you I'm still nursing a gut load
of Coco Pops Throbber asks if clitoral is a compound word
you know like toothpaste and I say I don't think so
since clitoral doesn't have anything to do with oral does it
and Fuckyou says of course it bloody does you arsenokoitai

when the geezer gets on I'm focusing down on my groin
who's lifting his lid at fantasy retinal splashes of Meena
fellating and I'm sure where the beast with two backs
is concerned she's got Shakespearean class (and her arse
yes her arse) and her scent is blown roses with hints of lime
like the memorial playground where I touched her hair
but she doesn't get on at her usual stop only the geezer
who's sweating Niagaras and blubbing a waterfall
pouring of prayer and it takes all sorts sniggers Throbber
and the geezer's bent double under a rucksack

so school prefect Fuckyou leaps up acting all keen puffs out
his badge like it's a Victoria Cross says take this seat here
the geezer's a goner eyes shrinking to annite in schist
but I'm thinking of Meena and the mole she has there
where cheekbone meets world only love in my heart
when white descends and air screams through silent lips
and metal dissolves on limbs on the scar of the rail
I'm fending off kisses of fire as I pass through the ghost
of double-glazed faces thrown in the window's eye look down
and see Fuckyou a turban of brain a crucifix body of nails

My Ex-boyfriend

Saturday afternoons I graced the bench
that gave onto the college cricket pitch.
He kissed me before going out to bat:
'For *Queen* and *girlfriend*,' always that charm, a gleam
in his eye where sport and adoration met.
Yes, he was beautiful, and I adored,
followed the path of each ball heavenward
into our future – kids, the whole dumb dream.
What can I say, that boy I loved is dead,
from something on the optic nerve, I heard,
inoperable, the size of a cricket ball.
But we're long history now. 'Sorry, old girl,'
he said one day, 'we're not going to make it.'
So I left him to his eight more years of cricket.

Sciophobia

He shambles in, demands they take the shadow
stalking his feet. I can't stand this shadow,

he shouts. It scares and alters me,
trails a weight of grey from me —

look there, where the floor is dark.
They tell him he must keep on through the dark

as this is just the way things are:
your shadow can tell you who you are.

Eating ciabatta in a North London café six days after the London bombs

Beyond the enormous *Welcome* sign
and soggy *Welcome* mat
Mario's all hours café is awake
in a dawn mist of its own percolated steam.

Mario himself greets me with a vigour
disproportionate to the early morning hour.
I take my seat by a row of ferns, stare out
at the North Circular's six a.m. rotating load,

at the row of sometimes bricked up,
sometimes done up Edwardian terraced houses
where the sensible city is still asleep.
A headscarved waitress takes my order.

Mario puts the toastie maker on.
Molecules of bacon loiter in the fug-air
over the counter, its plated pasties,
muscular croissants, sandwich towers.

He came to London, he once told me,
to marry his sweetheart.
Now he is shredding cabbage,
now he is at the griddle, at the board

chopping onions until his eyes flood.
Behind him the coffee machine
articulates his thirst for work.
A radio plays its universal anthems

of love and only last week's papers
spread out on a table speak of the bombs.
The waitress brings a plate of toasted ciabatta,
two gold bars of butter and a mug of tea,

specks of pink lipstick-glitter
on the edge of its white rim.
We talk of the ridiculous time of day,
of the weather. She asks what I'm reading,

laughs and says,' In the waking hour...!'
Outside the sun rises over cranes and decay,
illuminates the gold dome,
a bus stop down the road. In this light

there is purple in the wings of the pigeons
idling on the pavement. I raise the mug,
its hint of a smudge, towards my lips
and kiss a London stranger on the mouth.

Only thing can resolve conflict is love, like I felt for Fletch and Ruski, Spooner, and Calico. Pure love. What I feel for my cats present and past.

— William S Burroughs

Le chat
Je souhaite dans ma maison :
Une femme ayant sa raison,
Un chat passant parmi les livres,
Des amis en toute saison
Sans lesquels je ne peux pas vivre.

— Apollinaire

Missing

To the ceramic bowl
below the open window,
my cat who lapped its milk
rhythmically, with grace
each day for thirteen years,
does not return. I fill
the bowl to overflowing.

Search

Clang saucepans like bells,
rattle your lungs, holler
for townsfolk and all folk
to scour woodland, middens,
meads and byways for signs
he was there: blood on a thorn,
paw prints in clay or tar,
a risen warmth in the air.

Find the roaring ginger
of his fur, the pink carnation
of his anus, call down
the rook and the raven,
stir owls from their beds,
send your summons out
over fields and bridleways,
listen for his song, listen.

Maurice, Gone

I count the long days without you,
draw back the curtain where you swished
your hips and rubbed your neck
each morning against its folds.

I watch the flux outside, count the buds
that come and go, and find always
the same absence, a gap
on the lawn's sunny patch,

in the hollows of the flower bed
where your back uncurled, rolled,
each slender limb extended.
Where are you, Maurice? I love you.

Where did the road beyond our drive take you?
The house's threads contrive to bring you
home again: your presence reencountered
in a silk purse, an orchid's velvet bloom,

the restraint of a glass of milk. Your eyes,
reproachful, solemn, flood my amber brooch.
I hear your fractured purr inside a motor,
feel your tongue on my arm as I brush

the plywood door. I rub my cheek
against the door, would have that cheek bleed.
Here is a single blood-brown hair.
Here, vestiges of foot prints, crumbs of mud,

chaff and fluff, strands pulled loose
from a sofa back. I bury my face in the cushion
that holds you still, in the whiff of you,
the dust of you, the fur of you.

Imposter

As for the not-black-enough-
for-luck-cat from the Rectory
opposite, who sidles through
our window's chink to sup
from my tin of sockeye salmon,
who thinks it's acceptable
to unpick with her ten fine
needles the woollen stitches
of my grandmother's armchair,
she is not *my* cat. Spray her
with water from the iron. Shoo
her out*, now* — tinker, tailor, rich-
cat, poor-cat, beggar-cat, thief.

Poet-cat

Here's a tale for you, Maurice,
exactly nine lives long,
a didactic tale

in which the cat protagonist,
vacant and pensive
on his couch, teaches

the measure of each breath,
and gravity,
bliss in solitude.

Naming the cat

Upon their bodies and heads sit bats, swallows, and birds, and the cats also.
    – Baruch 6:21

We drive home with the new cat
confined in its wicker carrier
the day of the floods.
It mews through the gaps
the whole sullen journey .

Our house's stone hallways
drown, not in water,
but a kitten's ululations.
Bereft of his mother,
he's the eldest of the litter.

Kneeling at his basket
I soothe him with human purrs,
would name him Moses
if the Bible didn't underestimate
the importance of cats.

Part II

After the business of oversleeping, I apologise,

but I wish you could've known sleep like that,
and I was sure, for an hour or so, you were there,
deep in the dip by my side, curved loosely
round my body like a petal, your arm
above the pillow where it always is, your hand
touching my dream of Far Skerr dunes,
clouds over Lindisfarne streaked with light,
and I could've sworn it was your mouth on my face
that woke me, pulled me from my ammonite curl,
kissed me all the way downstairs only to find
you'd gone with your coat and your foot-stamp,
leaving that long-suffering look of yours
stuck to the fridge door with a magnet.

Your girlfriend's red leather jacket

It wasn't when we almost kissed at The Crowns
and her friend's look said, let the wicked
be ashamed, let them be silent in the grave.

It was when you lent me her red leather jacket
to walk through rain to The Moon and Stars,
her throat at the collar pleading, please, back off,

my elbow pushing out the hollow shaped by hers,
and under the top left pocket with her lipstick in
the beat of my heart fitting precisely the beat of hers.

Hanbury Street

I sailed into your top floor flat
on a crate labelled Handle with Care,
and everything was blue –
the walls, the doors, the linen
curtains your mother made,
the duvet like a small sea.

Through arched windows
we roped in colour, the sun's four poles –
a brick-red sofa longer than a body,
my orange penguin paperbacks, anthuriums,
the painting we couldn't afford
of fire burning over London,
burning up the blue.

St Bride's

The girl is walking towards him
in a taffeta silk wedding dress
stitched with sequins, little oyster beads,
trailing a patrimonial veil's
white Egyptian lace. She's trying,
down fifteen centuries of aisle, to bridge
the acreage between them, between her
and the rose that defines him,
uncurling warmly in his buttonhole.
Still sometimes shy with him, at least
she's learned he's kind, can stir a flame
from resolute cold. And yet to give a life,
fifty, maybe sixty, years on the back of that
seems – ridiculous. Twelve months ago
she didn't know his name, the satin scar
embroidered down a collarbone, the rapt
azure of his eyes when she unclips her hair,
or slides a limb beside him in the bed.
And now they're getting married,
her uncertainty hidden under layer
on layer of flounce, a corset's taut restraint.
When she comes close to his expectant face,
she thinks how little he knows of her,
how little anyone knows of anyone else.
The sun forces its way through coloured glass,
through the apostles in some parable.
She wonders if the dove above St Paul
aches for flight, or the alabaster angel
weighted to the nave. There are words
she wants to say, lines she has composed.
Tread softly, she wants to say, through the world

spinning through a ring's gold circle,
though she only echoes the priest, line
by line, each prescribed mouthful of vows.

Song

I meant to tell you how a song
can fill a body easily,
skirr upwards
towards the mind's longing
like poured water rising
in a naked glass,

how a song's shadow
can brush a thought of you,
who might be listening to it now
in a room alone somewhere
where music
and memory collide.

Wedding Gift

You gave me gold for my neck.
Its links linked
to make a constellation.

Newlywed, lightheaded,
I saw stars all that week,
in Connemara.

When I tripped and fell
on Binn Mhór's descent
the last day of our honeymoon

I didn't feel it break
or see a snake of sunlight
gulped by shade.

Rose

Though constantly moving, nomadic,
she's held by a white picket fence
to this square of garden where we,
through her, have rooted our world
for as long as it takes to raise a child.

Persuade her to stand still over there
where light strikes the puddled swing,
you'll see Pleiades freckle the tip
of her nose in June, jasmine
thread her yellow hair with white

as if she was made by stars and the sun,
not me, not us, not our small time
one night genetic accomplishment
that before she was born
we dared to call a mistake.

Get me started on her and it's hard to stop,
the birthmark like a moth,
reluctant hair, toes delicate
as pedicels — or, in the exact moment
the rose bush drops a bloom,

a sudden word-burst thrown to the lawn
and caught by us open-handed,
who can only guess at her language,
what kingdoms, myths
and creatures, what mysteries it holds.

The Eurythmics play 'Thorn in My Side'

When I asked what song reminds you of me
I should have guessed it wouldn't be Frankie's
'The Power of Love' or even Van Morrison's 'Brown Eyed Girl',
but somehow 'Thorn in My Side' seemed inappropriate
at that particular kissing moment,

so I took the Wilkinson Sword secateurs
your mother gave me for Christmas
to the mildewed Iceberg, the Sombreuil,
Wickwar, Souvenir de la
Malmaison and York and Lancaster —

from white to off-white shredded variously
before I came back inside
ready to smash your face
into the glass this side
of the snow and the huge roses.

The Waterboys play 'The Whole of the Moon'

The year we met, that summer driving
in your tin drum sports car from Abbraccio
del Lago to Dolcedo, music on, cigarette smoke
choking the open top and a glaze of alcohol
as golden as the light spilt over the road,

I remember thinking
we would never love like this again –
the settlement of early evening,
the easy smell of grass, the moon,
the whole damn white of it.

I held onto you those years ago
and now, on the same long Italian coast road,
I hold onto that slim translucent memory
the way the day will sometimes
hold onto the moon in its blue sky.

Emergency Birth

A cut like a needle's eye
and he's through – a boy! –
a five pound four ounce ravel of son
asserting breath, but holding on

by just the skin of his gums,
the small resolve of vernixed lungs
whispering *Yes* as his skin is a swab,
his throat a hole, a plastic tube.

Later she eavesdrops at his mouth
for life. Her T-shirt blots two clouds
as nearness spills her eager milk.
They say it'll take a miracle.

Inside her a kind of god-love lifts –
breathe, baby, keep breathing, live.

Heritage Dive

So we've found the world we swam from
at last, and I love it. The thrum

of almost silence coursing the reef
takes me back to the origin of life,

not my own cell-building spell in the womb,
but centuries ago, stromatolite time,

when that jellyfish orbiting
the sea fans, started perfecting his sting.

And you, my daughter, water-girl
bubbling out a comet trail

through full fathom blue, have pinched the DNA
of a goldtail angelfish (the hip sashay,

bold blue eyes, trailing yellow hair)
that set you on the path to here

and now, to you and me, cruising evolution
at minus altitude and going down...

And isn't that your father
over there, inside the big bald flounder?

The mussitation of the clam
seems to be mouthing: *Welcome home.*

Back

Naked in the bath, three years old,
his body folds to unfold
the map in the base of his back,
bringing to mind the precise moment
I created its pathways, its nerve-
wired comings and goings.

It was between Windemere and Devoke Water.
Eight weeks pregnant, hunched
over an Ordnance Survey map
in a route-search below sky larks
I blurted *There!* to the landscape
as my finger unhinged in discovery
on the crest of a vein-green path.

I'm sure I felt a shift of love
inside me, the cells of his back
move to their perfect slot,
a mole form on his spine like a small lake,
just then, when I found where we were
before turning off the bridleway
to take the footpath east to Coniston Water.

Mr Rice

Invulnerable, he thought, before the bank
collapsed, before losing his salary
and pension pot in one myopic blink.
Ordered to leave by noon, he stooped to pack
a cardboard box marked *Châteauneuf-du-Pape*
with the dregs of twenty sterling years: a pen
from a business trip to Cannes, a baseball cap
embroidered *Rice*, photos and drawing pins,
eight files, his legacy of stationery,
a mug embossed with *Boss*, a plant, his phone.
Briefly he laid his head on the desk — its stains,
its coffee rings and spattered pools of ink
bleeding from his mouth. Then he stood up,
picked up the box, steadied his lower lip,
walked out the door, damned if he'd look back.

Space

The distance between us is growing —
last month, love, you were in the heel
of the garden. I needed binoculars
to see you, as if you were some rare bird
whose song had caught my ear.

Last week you were overseas. I found you
on a screen, wandering tribal highways,
rubbing sand-storm from your eyes.
And tonight? — tonight I'm searching for you
through my telescope. Is that you up there

pacing the moon's white streets?
Our bedroom turns on its tragic axis
and the moon moves away from the earth.
Throw me a word on the back of a star,
quick, while the sky's still clear.

Family Man

Forget the paunch like a pregnancy,
the slowly eroding brim of hair, mysteriously
woven ball of greenish lint that infiltrates
the navel each evening. Forget the loo seats
hoiked up to attention, piles of shirts,
socks, dirty mugs itinerant over surfaces.

Look at him with his gold-haired son, the one
he skins like a rabbit love-trapped in the garden,
teaches the strength and weight of clay, of seeds
they plant like tiny dragon's teeth. At tea
he carries him over his shoulder into the house
like Jason with the golden fleece.

Loft

You told me to declutter,
clear out my head and junk –
binbagged clothes, a broken girandole,
a box of essays under a fur stole,
and a black briefcase full of the past
thrown up uninvited by our loft.
But I never thought I'd find
so many photos, note-scraps,
letters, Hallmark cards' forevers,
so much diarised desire.
Where are they now, those boy-men
who said they'd love until death?
They resurface now below bulb-glow
in my fluttering gut, like swallows.

Star Watch

My mother turned forty when I was twelve
and forty seemed as remote,
as unplaceable in my personal narrative,
as the stars I was trying to plot
with *Purnell's Concise Encyclopaedia*
and a short-sighted naked eye, and I was certain,
like the Crab Pulsar, I'd run out of hydrogen
or helium, collapse under gravity's burden
before reaching midlife's frontier.

Now, by lottery or zodiacal intent,
I'm at the brink, practically there,
an irritant tickle in the respiratory tract,
a bruised scapula, but otherwise intact,
and I view this as only a miniature
miracle: to have travelled *this far*
feet unsteady on the world's turning,
the whole ageing weight of me still burning.

Housework

This evening in the kitchen a man and a woman rowed.
As usual she was crying a little, no sobs, no hysteria.

As usual his arms were folded across his chest.
Their voices rose – the things they said! –

and their voices became subdued. Through the bay window,
the moon like someone intruding on their privacy.

When it was clear to them both it was pointless
to continue, they bent down together and emptied together

the dishwasher. Out came the glasses, the egg cups.
Out came the mugs: chipped, hairline cracked –

why wouldn't they be, twenty-three years of marriage?
And from the left side white ribs and right side

white ribs of the dishwasher
came the blue porcelain wedding present plates

like the scales of an old reptile, vivid, resilient,
stacked on the counter in two piles and put away.

From the heart of the carcass she drew the sharp knives
blade down in the cutlery basket, and attached them

to the metallic strip on the wall.
When they had emptied the cutlery from its basket

into the drawer, he came behind her and put his arms
around her waist and drew her towards him.

How glorious, to be held like that,
his little paunch in the small of her back,

her hands pulling his hands against the rolls of her belly,
the warmth of his cheek pressing through her hair,

and below them laid out messily
in the drawer, the knives, forks and spoons.

Alder

Hoof-pools brim, the berry hedgerows
unload the notes of birds whose names
I can't recall, and here's a ditch
that winter's shifted into lake
thieving the sky, a passing cloud,
the reflection of an alder tree
like a single cerebellum nerve cell.
I'm on the path to Horseshoe Hill
to get myself away from self.
It's clear these days I've been too much
inside, though the mind is a changing thing,
like naked alder drawn on water.

Sighting seals on a beach in the Farne Islands

It takes me back to a time when rocks
ruled the world in packs

and a day could last as long as a star
or the staid horizon for all creation cared

in that easier, previous life
of wordlessness, no currencies or human time,

with sea such as this —
wearing evening sky, these darks, carmines,

light bumping against tide as the wind draws in
and stirs our lonely boat to a shiver.

The Swan Hellenic Cruise

At the end of our small adventure
let us wake in a double cabin
wrapped in each other's shadow,
the air at our fingertips bright,
a porthole's pure iris.

May we know we never wanted
to be fiercely memorable, we stuck
to being ordinary, ruthlessly,
fellow travellers, however unsettled
the waves towards Ithaca.

October

These days I keep finding pieces of myself
lying around the house –

my swinging-out-of-bed foot
in the sock on the stairs,

my nerves
wound up in a ball of tights.

I was looking for a particular shirt,
I forgot what I was looking for,
I opened the washing machine, found my limbic zone
against the upper curve of the drum.

Look at my hands unwristed in a pair of gloves!

Paltry and damp,
is that what's left of me,

in the garden, pegged out on the line,
or is it all of us,
the whole nuclear family?

Notes

'Because I will be more American':
The phrase 'Big bird was strong and visual' draws on the
Wikipedia entry for the Format of *Sesame Street*.
The words in italics are from Bruce Springsteen's song
'Born in the USA'.
Line 43 From 'Napalm, from Harvard to Vietnam', by
Gal Beckerman, *The Boston Globe* (March 24, 2013).

'Overseas':
For Clare Medlicott (1989 – 2006)

'Walking the River Tay':
For Mark Finney

'Mosquito':
This poem takes its title from the poem by DH Lawrence
of the same name.
The epigram is also the epigram of the book *Mosquito* by
Andrew Spielman and Michael D'Antonio (Faber and
Faber, 2002) from which it is taken.
'Everything you do is all about you.' 'The romantic no-
tion of every creature having a vital place in nature may
not be enough to plead the mosquito's case.' Janet Fang
(*Nature* magazine, 21 July 2010).
'Such obscenity of trespass' is from the poem 'Mosquito'
by DH Lawrence.

'Three train stops from St. Francis Comprehensive':
For Adam Bruce-Gardyne: Kelso Place November 1989

'Sciophobia':
Line 8 From Stanley Cavell's essay 'The Avoidance of Love A Reading of King Lear' from his book *Must We Mean What We Say?* (Cambridge University Press, 1976).

'Missing':
After the first line of Kathleen Jamie's poem 'The Falcon', *The Tree House* (Picador, 2004).

'Imposter':
After the first line of Kathleen Jamie's poem 'The Cupboard', *The Tree House* (Picador, 2004).

'Poet-cat':
Lines 5-6 and 9 From 'Daffodils' by William Wordsworth.

'Family Man':
'To skin a rabbit' is a phrase meaning to remove a child's shirt or jumper by pulling it inside out over his or her head.

Acknowledgements

I'm grateful to the editors of the following publications where some of these poems or versions of them first appeared: *Acumen, Banshee, Coffee House Poetry, Letterpress Poets Anthology, Mslexia, South Bank Poetry,* and *The Rialto.*

'Three train stops from St Francis Comprehensive' won the 2015 Philip Larkin Poetry Prize.

'Emergency birth' was joint winner of the Ware Poetry Competition Sonnet Prize 2013 and 'After the business of oversleeping, I apologise' was highly commended in the Ware Poetry Competition 2013. Both were included in the *Ware Poetry Competition Anthology 2013.*

'Taking ciabatta in a North London café six days after the bombs' was commended in the 2014 South Bank Poetry Competition. '*Rattus Rattus*' won second prize in the Mslexia Poetry Competition 2013. 'Gorilla' was highly commended in the Essex Poetry Competition 2008 and 'Overseas' won the Essex Poetry Competition 2008.

'Heritage Dive' was longlisted for the 2012 National Poetry Competition.
'Because I will be more American' and 'Via del Corso' were both longlisted for the 2013 National Poetry Competition.

A number of poems or versions of poems appeared in my pamphlet *Drawn on Water* published by Eyewear in 2014 as part of their 20/20 series edited by Les Robinson.

I am grateful to Todd Swift for his generosity, energy and encouragement over many years. Mimi Khalvati has been a long term source of wisdom and support for which I am grateful. Huge thanks are due to Kathryn Maris and Sarah Wardle.

A number of people have offered encouragement and/ or commented on poems in this collection over the years and my thanks are due to all the members of my advanced poetry groups at Morley College and The Poetry School, to all at Letterpress Poets, to Tanya Barrett, Lisa Brockwell, James Flynn, Eric Fong, Frances Leviston, Mike Loveday, Roddy Lumsden, Don Paterson, Maurice Riordan, Les Robinson, Edwin Smet, Lucy Smith, Frances Spurrier, the Tudor family, Sarah Westcott and Kate White. Above all, thanks to Peter Pryor.

EYEWEAR PUBLISHING

EYEWEAR POETRY

MORGAN HARLOW MIDWEST RITUAL BURNING
KATE NOAKES CAPE TOWN
RICHARD LAMBERT NIGHT JOURNEY
SIMON JARVIS EIGHTEEN POEMS
ELSPETH SMITH DANGEROUS CAKES
CALEB KLACES BOTTLED AIR
GEORGE ELLIOTT CLARKE ILLICIT SONNETS
HANS VAN DE WAARSENBURG THE PAST IS NEVER DEAD
DAVID SHOOK OUR OBSIDIAN TONGUES
BARBARA MARSH TO THE BONEYARD
MARIELA GRIFFOR THE PSYCHIATRIST
DON SHARE UNION
SHEILA HILLIER HOTEL MOONMILK
FLOYD SKLOOT CLOSE READING
PENNY BOXALL SHIP OF THE LINE
MANDY KAHN MATH, HEAVEN, TIME
MARION MCCREADY TREE LANGUAGE
RUFO QUINTAVALLE WEATHER DERIVATIVES
SJ FOWLER THE ROTTWEILER'S GUIDE TO THE DOG OWNER
TEDI LÓPEZ MILLS DEATH ON RUA AUGUSTA
AGNIESZKA STUDZINSKA WHAT THINGS ARE
JEMMA BORG THE ILLUMINATED WORLD
KEIRAN GODDARD FOR THE CHORUS
COLETTE SENSIER SKINLESS
BENNO BARNARD A PUBLIC WOMAN
ANDREW SHIELDS THOMAS HARDY LISTENS TO LOUIS ARMSTRONG
JAN OWEN THE OFFHAND ANGEL
A.K. BLAKEMORE HUMBERT SUMMER
SEAN SINGER HONEY & SMOKE
RUTH STACEY QUEEN, JEWEL, MISTRESS
HESTER KNIBBE HUNGERPOTS
KEATON HENSON IDIOT VERSE
MEL PRYOR SMALL NUCLEAR FAMILY
ELIZA STEFANIDI SLEEPING WITH PLATO

EYEWEAR PROSE

SUMIA SUKKAR THE BOY FROM ALEPPO WHO PAINTED THE WAR
ALFRED CORN MIRANDA'S BOOK
MARIO BELLATIN THE LARGE GLASS

EYEWEAR LITERARY CRITICISM

MARK FORD THIS DIALOGUE OF ONE - WINNER OF THE 2015 PEGASUS AWARD
FOR POETRY CRITICISM FROM THE POETRY FOUNDATION (CHICAGO, USA).